Ray Reardon was born in a small mining town in South Wales. He had been a miner and a policeman before devoting himself to the game of snooker, and there were many years of disappointment before he reached the top as an amateur and – later still – a professional player of international acclaim. He won the world championship six times against an increasing challenge and became the snooker colossus of the seventies.

RAY
REARDON
BEDSIDE
SNOOKER

Fore!

ILLUSTRATIONS
BY
COLIN WHITTOCK

Fontana/Collins

First published by Century Publishing Co. Ltd 1983
First issued in Fontana Paperbacks 1984

Copyright © in text Ray Reardon 1983
Copyright © in drawings Colin Whittock 1983

Cover photograph by Huston Spratt
Editor Michael Leitch
Designed by David Pocknell's Company Ltd
Production Reynolds Clark Associates Ltd

Made by Lennard Books,
Mackerye End,
Harpenden, Herts AL5 5DR

Printed and bound by
William Collins Sons & Co. Ltd, Glasgow

CONTENTS

SNOOKER CRAZY

Behind every successful snooker pro, gliding aristocratically beneath the TV lights in his sharkskin waistcoat and brilliantined shoes – sport's answer to Fred Astaire (and sexy with it) – stands an unseen army. The fans. In their way, the fans are crazier about snooker than the pro. Many of them are recent converts, drawn into the web via the magic of *Pot Black* and colour television; some play a bit, and some are wholly content to watch.

There is, though, another, wilder regiment in snooker's gallant army. It is manned by lads of all ages from seventeen to seventy-nine, and their distinguishing mark (if you ask them) is that they too have had a taste of glory at the table. Their regimental motto is: 'Who knows?' Who knows, had they practised just a tiny bit more often (say once a week), had they drunk a few less gallons of beer (just a few), had they not missed the black that night Joe Davis came to the club (it *nearly* went in), why, word would have got round, wouldn't it? Bound to. The sky would have been the limit. Who knows?

Yes, the professional knows all about these lads, the heroes and villains of the amateur leagues. He started there himself, after all, and not so very long ago. In fact, if you want to hear the true life story of a *typical* snooker player, it goes something like this . . .

A STAR IS BORN

Or so his mother maintains. (His father is down at the Institute having a quick game and is unavailable for comment.) Other relatives, neighbours and friends clustering round the pram in the narrow High Street are not certain they are in the presence of a prodigy, but all crane eagerly over the tiny sleeping figure, making his first public outing. He wakes, and soon a gasp runs through the crowd.

'Look,' cries the babe's Aunt Gladys, 'it's true! Look at his eyes!'

All can confirm the truth of the rumour: the boy indeed has one red eye and one white. The Omen! But Mrs Fosdyke

Aaagh! One red and one white behind the black – 'tis an omen...

from No 33 is not convinced. She sniffs:

'Suppose he's just been crying a lot? Doesn't prove anything!' She gives the multitude the benefit of her 'superior' look.

While Mrs Fosdyke is trying simultaneously to outstare Aunt Gladys and Mother, up sidles Uncle Fred, Father's older brother. He pushes his way to the front and peers down at the baby, then, after nodding as though satisfied by what he has seen, brings out a billiard cue from behind his back and lays it gently on the child's blanket.

'It's one I had when I was a lad,' Uncle Fred explains to the others, a little hoarsely, clearing his throat in an embarrassed way. The slim fag-end between his lips has gone out and he bangs his coat pockets for matches.

Down in the pram, the white eye swivels towards the red as the baby focuses on his uncle's blessed gift. Then with a cry and a chuckle the baby seizes the cue at the point of balance, raises it high and with a lusty swing uses it to bat Mrs Fosdyke in the bosom before she can do so much as raise her handbag in self-defence.

A murmur of satisfaction runs through the crowd, drowning Mrs Fosdyke's cries of pain and alarm. Uncle Fred smiles benevolently down.

'Go get her, boy,' he breathes through his fag-end, adding, 'lovely grip', that, an' all.'

AT THE INSTITUTE

His first snooker table measures four feet by two. He is soon master of the basic techniques, though hampered to begin with because the balls are too big for the holes. He switches to large marbles instead, with instant success. At school he is famed for his accuracy with a peashooter. When threatened by a teacher for shooting a pea into another boy's ear at fifteen paces, he indignantly replies: 'It's not my fault, is it, if he's got ears like billiard pockets?'

At the Institute, mainly in the school holidays, Uncle Fred finds him a box to stand on and instructs him in the finer arts every weekday afternoon. By the age of eleven he is winning money for Uncle Fred, whose usual terms against known opponents are 'Sixpence a game and ten/fifteen/twenty points for the lad.' In the next end-of-term school report his attendance rating drops from 'Fair' to 'Does he know we too are open in the afternoon?' Mother throws a big scene, so he shelves his great plan to run away to London and turn professional.

If you lose, you give him sixpence *and* do his homework!

TRAINEE SHARK

He enters instead for a regional boys' tournament and suffers his first
setback: a seven-year-old from the next town gives him a severe
drubbing. Back to the practice table. At fourteen he wins selection for
the Valley and District League team and becomes a regular player. He
is viewed as a good prospect but his team-mates are sparing with their
praise, not wishing him to become big-headed; nor are they keen to
sacrifice their own places in the eight-man team. He leaves school and
goes to work in a garage. Now he is a regular face at the Arcadia
Billiards & Snooker Club, upstairs from the menswear shop in the High
Street. On Saturdays he is picking up two or three pounds for winning
sixpenny games of skittles pool, Russian pool and scrub. He is
nicknamed Redeye, and his performances at the table attract the
attention of Jimmy the Shark, the craftiest player in town. At a price,
he learns from Jimmy the financial benefits of playing a tight game, of
letting the opponent make the crucial first mistake.

Girls take second place to snooker practice. Even
boozing with the lads at the Asphaltlayers Arms is rationed to the last
half hour of the evening, so he can squeeze in extra practice and stay
ahead of the pack. He quits the garage and, to save time commuting to
and from the Arcadia, he scrubs his fingernails and lands a job on the
Tie and Handkerchief counter at the menswear shop. He celebrates his
first payday at the shop by lashing out on a huge bow-tie in maroon
velvet that he has lusted after all week. By then he has realized, too late,
that working in a shop means he cannot be free to join the Saturday
gambling sessions at the Arcadia much before 5.32 pm, but he
compensates for this by forming a Retailers & Allied Trades
competition, which meets at the Arcadia on early-closing days and
which he dominates.

TOP OF THE LEAGUE

His canny game makes him the best player in the League team, as well
as the best-dressed since no-one else ever wears a tie, even for away
matches. The committee begin to consider him as a future captain, but
prudently decide to wait on the grounds that no-one has previously
made it to captain under the age of forty-six. Meanwhile, he can always
be counted on to win his two frames in League matches. His consistent
form bucks up the other team members and they crown a triumphant
year by carrying off the League trophy. Though a great success at local
level, Redeye has trouble making progress in tournaments; his biggest
success is to reach the second round of the English under-eighteen

championship. He still practises hard, but also manages to find time to down six pints at the local where he used to be content with three.

He is just turned twenty-one when green-eyed ex-Bathing Queen Angie Boyd joins the staff of the bank across the road from the menswear shop. Gazing out from behind the dummies, Redeye is instantly enslaved. A friend on the local newspaper introduces them. Click!

You'll have to marry me now!

THE TROPHY WON AND LOST

Beer and Angie mean that snooker now commands only one-third of his leisure time. Each evening he must rush between the Arcadia, the Asphaltlayers Arms and the canal bank if he is to keep his hand in at all three activities. Marriage to Angie tilts the balance even further away from snooker, and Angie's special way with steak and kidney puddings rapidly adds about a foot to his already burgeoning waistline.

He still manages to practise once a week and holds his place in the League team, but he can no longer be relied on to win either of his two frames. Angie's pregnancy means that he is required to stagger beside her carrying the groceries on his free afternoons. Fortunately, his loss of earnings from not gambling in midweek does not affect the family income level since he had already developed the habit of splurging his winnings on booze all round before going home.

Despite his patchy League form, he wins through to the final of the Arcadia's annual trophy competition, to be staged on the last Friday night before Christmas. This year the club is celebrating its fiftieth year, and a famous Welsh professional has agreed to present the trophy and play an exhibition match with the winner.

The day of the final begins badly for Redeye. The bitter the night before had been cloudy, but Angie offers no sympathy saying that his belly is bigger than hers anyway, and she is eight months pregnant. He storms off to work and endures a slow and gastrically turbulent morning. At lunch he is angry and sulky as well as thirsty, so stays in the pub until closing time. By late afternoon his already queasy stomach is assailed by pre-match nerves, and he pops out to the off-licence for half a bottle of alcoholic peppermint which he consumes in the store-room. Since breakfast he has only eaten two packets of cheese and onion crisps but when the shop closes he decides that further food might a) be difficult to keep down, or b) make him feel sleepy. He just has time to top up with five more pints before the match. He rings home from the pub to make his peace with Angie, and get her to wish him luck, but there is no reply.

If just one of you two hits form we'll smash that Welsh blighter!

Redeye is looking forward to the contest, regardless of his uneven personal build-up to it. He has already decided that the Arcadia trophy is as good as won. Charlie Pink, his opponent, has never beaten him in the seven years they have played each other. It is the Welsh pro that Redeye is after. 'If I can smash that bloke,' he urges himself in the club toilet, 'who knows where it will lead to?' Later, in the mirror, he treats himself to a fierce look. 'This is the big one, boy. You better be good tonight.'

Redeye and Charlie Pink are introduced to the Welsh professional and the final begins: best of seven frames. Redeye surges ahead and takes the first three frames. As Charlie breaks for the fourth frame, Redeye gives the Welsh pro one of his meanest looks, as if to say: 'Your turn next, big shot.' Oddly, though, Charlie takes the fourth frame and the fifth. During the sixth, Redeye begins to feel light-headed and a wave of nausea passes over him as he waits to play. Charlie wins again. 3–3. In the final frame Redeye again feels unsteady and has to hang on to the cushion several times to support himself. His play is deteriorating but fortunately, under the stress of the occasion, so is Charlie's. Eventually, the championship hangs on the final black, with Redeye to play.

The importance of the moment has sharpened Redeye's concentration. He steps up, gets into position and goes straight into the shot. His cue performs an inelegant swerve, and the black misses the pocket by a clear two inches; slowly it rolls back to rest precisely on its spot. Redeye cannot believe it. His eyes bulge horribly as he suddenly sees the biggest chance of his life ebbing away to vanishing point . . . no trophy, no exhibition match with the Welshman, no nothing. Only disgrace. In a fit of wild rage and resentment he grabs the errant black ball from the table, turns, and with a bellow of anger hurls it through one of the massive windows overlooking the High Street.

'Bloody ba-aa-aa-ll!' he shouts after it.

Almost before the cascade of broken glass has hit the pavement, the shocked committee are on their feet. An impromptu interval is declared, and the Welsh pro, who appears to be trying hard not to laugh, is hustled rapidly out to the steakhouse down the road.

Later, the match is awarded to Charlie Pink. Redeye is barred from the Arcadia for six months.

CHANGE AND DECAY

Years pass, three children arrive, and Angie shows her real concern for Redeye's vastly swollen gut by persuading him to switch to vodka. He is astonished by the ease of the changeover, and soon he can get by on 1.5 litres of drink per day instead of a gallon and a half. What a wonderful wife and mother! The effect on his snooker is less beneficial. The hand on the table is the first to develop an uncontrollable twitch, and this is followed in the space of six months by a similar affliction of the hand holding the cue. When both twitches are on the go, they seldom do so in tandem, and it becomes very difficult to decide when to try and strike the cue ball. He loses his place in the League team to a twelve-year-old computer enthusiast. A break of 16 is his best score in the first calendar year of the vodka regime, but in his heart he knows it would be folly to go back on the beer. He decides to put his faith in defensive play and soldiers on, even though it is becoming harder to find opponents prepared to put up with his eternal safety shots, and frames lasting for two hours. His fortieth birthday passes. Next week he is fifty. No-one calls him Redeye anymore, since it is generally agreed that his white eye is now so bloodshot it is impossible to distinguish between them.

The hair is beginning to fall out, and if one is found on a ball it is usually his. The days are long gone when he could cock one knee up on the table to play a shot. The eyes are going as well; even with his new spectacles he has trouble telling the brown from the reds. During a particularly bad game he is inclined to look down the side of the club room where the old fogeys and visitors sit. Soon he'll be spending his days sitting it out on one of those benches. Still, it could be worse, and at least Angie doesn't mind him going down to the club. Now that snooker is so popular on television, she is pleased to know that her husband associates with such well-dressed, gentlemanly, non-violent people. He'll drink to that.

He could have been good if he hadn't misspent his youth – the bloody fool found a job and got married!

THE PLAYER'S GUIDE TO BODY MAINTENANCE

S nooker is a night game. For the professional, who learned his trade playing matches at night, this is the most natural time to go into action. His body and mind are geared to a nocturnal timetable and, until recently, he lived for most of the year like someone on permanent late shift. Nowadays the tournaments are much bigger than they were but for various reasons they must be completed in the same number of days. At first this meant playing in the afternoons as well. Now there is a morning shift too, beginning at 10.30. It has all been a bit hard on the poor old players' metabolisms. Never the most athletic of sportsmen, they have found it difficult to adapt to drinking, smoking and playing at full nervous pitch for more than twelve hours at a time.

I know, I know! I can hear the protests of my colleagues even as I write this. But as a professional body we must accept our responsibilities. The new gruelling schedules are not going to go away in a hurry, and some of us (no names) will have to mend our ways and toughen up. With this in mind, I have assembled some medical notes which I hope will be the basis for a new, leaner, fitter breed of snooker professional.

SLEEP

This, and the related difficulty of getting to bed, is the biggest problem of all. After an evening's play, finishing at 10.30 or 11pm, autographs must be signed, then it's off to the bar for a session with the other players or the committee. Before the player can turn round, it's 1am. He gets to bed at 2 o'clock, but still is not sufficiently relaxed or wound down. He falls asleep around 4 o'clock, and wakes up with a thick head in a hot stuffy hotel room twenty minutes after they have stopped serving breakfast.

Dr Ray's medical tip This player is staying in the wrong hotel. When making a reservation, he should find a hotel where there are no other snooker players in residence. He should avoid, in particular, Welsh, Irish, English, Scottish, Canadian and Australian snooker players.

EATING

LADA CARS
SNOOKER
CLASSIC

Too late for breakfast, the player shaves and drags his empty stomach to the hotel car park. It is a six-hour drive to the next venue. He cannot stop on the motorway for something to eat because he won two televised tournaments last year and every café contains at least a dozen people who will want to dip their biscuit in his tea and shout 'Sign this napkin.' He arrives at the next town but is snared in the evening rush-hour traffic for thirty minutes. At the hotel it is too early for dinner, so he settles for a cup of coffee and a plate of sandwiches. He could wait another hour for a cooked meal, but he knows that if he eats a big meal less than ninety minutes before a match he gets a bit sleepy, too contented for pro snooker. In the bar after the match, around 12.15am, he feels hungry so someone brings him . . . a plate of sandwiches. In a way, he prefers this to the late-night cooking – Indian or Chinese – available in that town; the taste of chapattis reminds him of a rusk that has been in someone's back pocket for a fortnight, and he is convinced that the Chinese are permanently constipated from eating all that rice ('You've only got to look at their squinty eyes'). So he goes to bed only having eaten two lots of sandwiches all day.

Dr Ray's medical tip This player should seriously consider buying a motorized caravan. Then he could do all his own cooking in the back. Think what fun that would be.

.EXERCISE

If he is feeling flush enough to stay in a hotel with a swimming pool, he likes a late-morning dip. He has always loathed running, reckoning that he is built not for speed, but to last. With some friends he founded an exclusive golfers' association, but has not played for three years because he is never in one place long enough, or too fragile in the mornings.

Dr Ray's medical tip Eight hours' uninterrupted rest will do much more good than violent exercise which, with someone as unfit as he is, can only increase the risk of a premature end.

DRINK

Coping with the booze is an eternal problem but there are some days when he thinks he has cracked it and can glide through a day's tournament play feeling no pain whatsoever. On rough nights, he has cause to bless the 'drink and drive' laws. These allow him to decline the committee's offer of unlimited whiskies in favour of a fruit juice – and to do so without causing offence. 'Oh, quite, I quite understand,' says the chairman of the committee, slipping his own treble quickly on to a side table. 'Very good of you to point it out.' And the time it would have taken – usually several hours – to drink the unlimited whiskies is cut to half an hour while he drips the fruit juice into his system, says goodbye, goes back to his hotel and has a quiet drink there, just him and the barmaid. If the bar is shut he can always order a drink, or there may even be a bar-fridge to play with in his room.

Dr Ray's medical tip Players should avoid opening bar-fridges if they have already been drinking for more than five hours continuously, as can happen at well-sponsored tournaments. Otherwise, bar-fridges are an excellent invention.

BAR FRIDGE

Nice to see the lads are feeling normal, isn't it?

STRESS

When he is playing well, he needs a large dose of pre-match stress to charge him up for the occasion; otherwise he loses interest and may then play badly. He actually enjoys the excitement of waiting to go on and play, especially if there is a large crowd. If there is a large crowd out there *and* television cameras, he laps it up; he can sit for hours in his room grinning at the reflection coming up from his dress shoes. When he is going through a bad spell, however, his hands shake and he needs several drinks before he can even practise.

Dr Ray's medical tip This player is perfectly normal.

HI-DE-HI!

The holiday-camp circuit has been good for snooker professionals. Good because the camps keep us busy when the tournament season is over. Good also because the atmosphere there is much more happy-go-lucky, which helps us to keep our sense of humour and not grow too self-important.

What can you do but laugh, after all, when you have lined up your shot and are just about to play it when a small hand comes over the side of the table and snatches the object ball?

'Mum! Mum!' shouts the owner of the hand, rushing away. 'Look what I've found!'

The first few times this happens you have to restrain an impulse to belt him with your cue, but you get used to it. 'Keep smiling through', as they say. Another time, you may be shooting into a far pocket. You are down over the table, concentrating hard; you glance up once more at the pocket, and two eyes are staring at you through the mesh. Now you need all the icy calm of a Grand Master as you rifle the ball into the pocket, aiming for a point in the centre of the small spectator's forehead.

Yes, it's all very friendly at the holiday camps; no point in being pompous. Not when eighty per cent of the tables look more like upland pastures for sheep than playing surfaces for snooker.

One table I shall never forget had the shakes. Instead of eight legs stout and true, this table was supported in such a way that every time a player put his weight on it, the playing surface moved and all the balls started to wobble. The knack with this table was to line up your shot and then wait. You waited until the cue ball and the object ball were wobbling in the same direction. Then you quickly played your shot before the wobble pattern changed. Simple really.

Usually at a holiday camp the table is in the Games Room, alongside various other facilities for darts, table tennis, and so on. In the winter, when the camp is closed, the table gets damp and

The table will be free in a moment, Mr Reardon – when we have judged the junior sand-dancing contest.

starts to warp. The cushions get even soggier than they were the year before. A new cover is a rare thing indeed; the old one gets older, but is never brushed or ironed. The pockets may be too small. I fully expect to arrive at a holiday camp some day to find all the pockets blocked with signs saying 'Closed for Repairs.'

Still, never mind. Here you are again, all set to play the weekly winners in the camp's senior and junior competitions. At least, you console yourself, you have brought your own cue, whereas your opponents mostly rely on the house specials. These are made in Taiwan and are about as straight as shepherd's crooks.

The main problem, though, is the playing surface. You can hit the ball perfectly, but it will not go in. Miss a few like that, and the knowledge-boxes in the audience will start to shake their heads.

Of course, you're at a disadvantage having a proper cue.

'He missed that,' one of them will point out, with perfect accuracy, to his mate.

'He should have got that,' his mate replies.

You settle down for your next shot just as a fresh mob of spectators arrive from the bar, glasses in hand. A waitress clatters past with a tray of empties. The door bangs. You hit another perfect shot but the object ball reacts as if it has hit quicksand, braking sharply several inches short of the pocket. In the silence that follows you pray that one of the knowledge-boxes will not start tut-tutting.

Tut-tutting has a bad effect on you. It makes the hair on the back of your neck rise up in prickles. It also gives you a rapidly mounting desire to stuff your cue up the knowledge-box's nose.

But that would never do. 'Be friendly,' you remind yourself constantly. 'Keep smiling through.' You compromise by shaking your head and forcing a rueful grin to spread over your face, even though what you really feel like doing is packing it in and going off for a round of golf.

I said a decent player can play on any table...

'He missed that one, an' all,' says a voice, loudly enough for you to hear. You are, of course, *meant* to hear. The point is, he is annoyed with you, and wants you to know that. He has given up half an hour's sunbathing by the swimming pool, or even a half-day Mystery Coach Tour, to come and watch you play your exhibition match. And you repay him by missing your shots. He is beginning to have serious doubts about whether you can play. As every non-playing snooker expert knows, if the balls don't go in, the man can't play.

It is fatal, of course, to try to defend yourself. Within seconds the air will be thick with wise old sayings to the effect that a bad workman always blames his tools, that those who can't stand the heat should get out of the kitchen, etc., etc.

COLD BALLS

The great secret with audiences – however knowledgeable or otherwise they may be – is to *retain the initiative*. Alex Higgins was playing an exhibition match in Lancashire when he decided that his game was being adversely affected because the balls were too cold. He complained, and asked the organizers to warm the balls for him.

It is a fact that snooker balls play better if they are not stone cold or damp. Appreciating this, the organizers removed all twenty-two balls from the table and put them on a nearby hot-water pipe. Then Alex played another game, but still he was not satisfied that the balls were warm enough.

'No,' he said firmly. 'They're no good.' He turned and pointed towards the bar. 'I want them in the pie machine.'

Up on the bar stood a large machine for heating pies and other hot snacks. The bar steward was called over, and he began emptying the machine of pies and stacking them on the bar. When the machine was empty, in went the snooker balls. For the next ten minutes the snooker balls lay snugly cooking on the trays inside the pie machine, while about eighty pies stood rapidly cooling on the bar.

After pulling a stroke like that, Alex had the audience exactly where he wanted them. No-one would have dared criticize him after that. Clearly, the man was in a mood to put *them* in the pie machine!

Ah, that's better!

NEVER MIND
THE WEATHER

There are quite a few encyclopedias of sports and games in the bookshops nowadays. But not all of them have an entry on either billiards or snooker. Funny, I thought, the first time I noticed this; I decided to ask some questions. The reason, I found, is that the publishers of these books on sports and games like to split the subject into separate volumes on indoor and outdoor games. According to them, billiards and snooker are indoor games, so they only put them in the indoor volume.

Personally I am not happy with this arrangement. I would prefer to see separate entries for billiards and snooker in *both* volumes. To ignore the outdoor aspects of these games is to take a very narrow view of them. Any professional worth his salt must know, for instance, how to play on a rain-soaked table. It is part of the job. At Manchester in 1974 Fred Davis must have wished he had wipers fitted on his spectacles as the rain spattered down through a gap in the roof. Some builders had been doing renovation work up there in the week before the tournament, and had left parts of the roof only lightly covered with plastic sheeting. Fred found it increasingly hard to concentrate. The balls were sending up spray like motor boats, the cloth was turning a very dark shade of green, and eventually, when he could not see across to the other side of the table, Fred asked the referee to call a halt. The referee, obviously a sympathetic man, agreed.

Fred was lucky. When a similar thing happened to me in 1982, my opponent and the referee treated me as if I had gone potty.

We were at the Derby Assembly Rooms. Tony Knowles was in play and I was sitting in my corner when I began to feel wet spots hitting the back of my hand. I looked up and saw a fine drizzle falling from the roof. No, I thought. Can't be. This is an indoor tournament. It can't be rain. But it was. And I was getting wet. I decided to tell the referee, so I went over to him.

'It's raining,' I said.

'Oh, yes,' he said, showing little interest.

'I'm not kidding you,' I said. 'It's raining.'

'Come off it,' he said.

I looked up. He was right. It was not raining. It had stopped. I must be going loony, I thought, and went back to my seat. A couple of seconds later, I looked up at the roof. There it was: rain. It was definitely raining. I went over to Tony Knowles at the table and said:

'Excuse me, Tony. I know it's very wrong of me to interrupt you when you're in play. But it's raining.'

He gave me an odd, questioning look; the look of a man who clearly thinks it is not raining.

'Honestly,' I said. 'It's raining.'

Each time I said it, only to be met with rebuffs and strange looks, it sounded lamer and more improbable than the time before. Was I perhaps reaching the end of the road?

As we stood there, the TV people started to show interest. They wanted to know what the mystery was so they could tell the viewers. I called everyone over to my seat, and we gathered round it. It was raining.

'There,' I said.

They agreed. Where we stood, it was raining. But nowhere else. It was not raining next to the table, or on the other side of the table; only where I had been sitting.

Someone offered the theory that there might be a small hole in the roof. I am not so sure about that. It seems more likely to me that it was a message. From up there. You know. Trying to *tell* me something.

SNOOKER WITH ELEPHANTS

In Canada snooker is mostly played indoors – probably because of the climate – but they also have a hybrid version which is played outdoors in a marquee. I had a go at this once at the Canadian National Exhibition in Toronto, which is a kind of circus-festival with the most extraordinary mixture of events and attractions I have ever seen.

It lasts for about three months and is staged in a vast park. There are stalls and marquees for everything that can be put

Foul stroke! I trust the human cannonball didn't put you off, Mr Reardon?

under a roof: circus acts, bands, sideshows, food stalls galore. Plus air displays, and cannons that fire once an hour. You are in your marquee trying to play snooker against a constant background cacophony of elephants trumpeting, a steel band playing, aircraft zooming overhead. Bang! Bang! There go the cannons again.

Then the rain begins to fall. Not just an average British drizzle, a massive Canadian downpour. Soon water is running under the table and we have to play standing on pallets. Water is cascading in through holes in the roof. It is all right for the spectators, who have come prepared. They just hoist their umbrellas inside the marquee and carry on watching.

Looking back, I suppose it was all very challenging and interesting; but to me the best news was that I did not have to stay for the full three months!

ON THE RED GROUND

In Tredegar, where I was born, the men settled their disputes on a shale patch about 700 feet up the mountainside, known as the Red Ground. If you fell out with someone, you didn't start scrapping there and then. You would agree a time to meet up on the Red Ground and settle your differences there. Most of the male population of Tredegar enjoyed watching a good fight, and this civilized way of organizing things gave them plenty of time to walk up and see the action.

Another native of Tredegar, and a great snooker rival, is Cliff Wilson. BBC Wales decided to join the two elements in a programme celebrating the rise to fame of Welsh snooker professionals. They persuaded Cliff and me to stage a snooker duel on the Red Ground; they also roped in Terry Griffiths to be the referee and had Doug Mountjoy acting as a second.

Oh, and a nice 147 maximum would be good for the viewers...

Their next problem was to get a snooker table up to the Red Ground. A full-sized table, with five slates, must weigh about one and a half tons, so they had a lot of fun lugging it up the slope and trying to find somewhere to stand it for our match. In the end it was decided to have one side of the table sticking out in a horizontal direction from the slope; this side was propped up with blocks.

'Fine,' we all said, then someone realized that the base of this sticking-out side was about three feet lower than the other side. To play a shot on that side, you didn't need a rest so much as a crane to lift you into position.

Unlike in the old days, when a fair crowd could be guaranteed to come and watch a fight, our contest was viewed only by a dozen or so sheep and two horses. It had rained the day before filming, it rained while the table was being installed, and during the game itself conditions could only be described as cold, damp, drab and miserable. Still, as you know, we snooker players will do anything to be seen on television in our dress suits. How else can you explain the spectacle of Wilson and Reardon slithering about on a wet mountainside, attended by Griffiths and Mountjoy blowing on blue fingers and praying for a quick finish? I'll tell you how. Patriotism. That's what it was. Rugged Welsh patriotism. Hadn't thought of that, had you? No, nor did we till after!

BAD LIGHT STOPPED PLAY

The bulb exploded with a flash and a pop, and the bits came raining down on the table, singeing the cloth and filling the air with the kind of smell which makes people want to give up smoking in bed. The audience gibbered nervously like a tribe of savages surprised by a partial eclipse of the sun. The BBC men cursed quietly, and began looking for a replacement bulb for their lighting system. The players also cursed quietly, knowing there would be a delay of at least an hour while a new cloth was fitted, during which time the adrenalin would seep out of their systems, leaving them to make a cold and doubly nervous start.

The television lights do not fail all that often but when they do, and the table is damaged, the effect is not at all the same as when a bulb at home gives up the ghost. There, you stick in a new one and carry on. At a snooker tournament the problem is not the bulb, but the table.

Because a full-sized table is so heavy and bulky, there is little hope of just wheeling in a new one. Snooker tables have to be taken apart before they will pass through the average door, and the job of lifting them is roughly as awkward as shunting Columbia out to the launch-pad for its next voyage. So the usual remedy is to fit a new cloth, which is no easy task and takes about an hour to complete.

I remember one occasion when the BBC *did* wheel in a snooker table. It was at the Sports Personality of the Year ceremony after Terry Griffiths had won the world championship, and a table was brought in so he could play a few shots. The producers had mounted the table in advance on a trolley, and this meant that when it was in position in the studio it was about six inches too high for Terry. Even a difference of half an inch would be noticed by a professional, so Terry had a difficult time ahead of him, trying to show why he, out of all the sports personalities present, deserved to win the award. Fortunately, he coped very well. All the same, it might have been better if they had offered to put *him* on a trolley as well!

SPOT THE HABIT

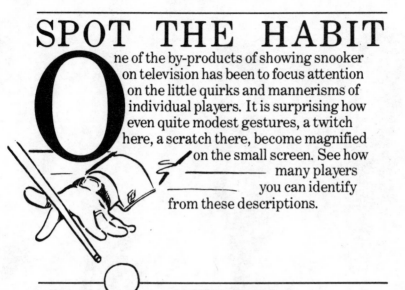

One of the by-products of showing snooker on television has been to focus attention on the little quirks and mannerisms of individual players. It is surprising how even quite modest gestures, a twitch here, a scratch there, become magnified on the small screen. See how many players you can identify from these descriptions.

QUESTIONS

When he smokes a cigarette, he holds it delicately between thumb and forefinger, like a puff pastry, drawing on it in the most genteel fashion. Who is he?

When he smokes a cigarette, he attacks it with huge drags, as if he is trying to propel shafts of smoke through the back of his head. Who is he?

Who sniffs all the time he is at the table?

Who plays with his head cocked at an 'impossible' angle halfway down one side of the cue?

Who has the flashiest waistcoats in the game?

Whose middle finger taps up and down on the table while he is playing a shot?

Which right-handed player keeps his chalk in his left waistcoat pocket, and has to perform a small juggling act, transferring cue and chalk from hand to hand each time he wants to apply a fresh coat of chalk?

Who loves jelly babies?

Who grinds his cue into the chalk so hard you can see little mounds of chalk dust piling up on the floor at his feet?

ANSWERS

The smokers are, respectively, Terry Griffiths and Alex Higgins.

The sniffer is John Spencer. At first we used to think he had a cold. Then we thought it must be something else – unless he had a cold every day of the year. Then we noticed he only sniffed when he was at the table.

Graham Miles is the contortionist. We can not understand how he manages to see what he is doing, but there is a theory going round that he has a third eyeball in his left ear!

Waistcoats are getting brighter all the time, but I reckon the South African Perrie Mans has the most colourful collection on the circuit.

The 'piano player' is John Virgo.
The man with the chalk-and-cue routine is . . . me.
All that changing of hands may look daft, and many people have been kind enough to point out that I would not have to do it if I kept the chalk in my right waistcoat pocket. But there is a reason. If the chalk is in the right pocket, it bulges out just enough to catch against my right thumb as I play a shot. So I have to keep the chalk somewhere else. I could put it in my right trouser pocket, of course, but that would be too easy, wouldn't it?

Alex Higgins loves jelly babies.
The big chalk merchant is Cliff Thorburn. We call him The Herculean Chalker.

ODDBALLS

You can blame the player most of the time, but there are some occasions when snooker balls – regardless of class, creed or colour – take on a life of their own. In a famous example, repeatedly shown on television, it was the blue ball that went mad. Instead of going into the pocket, it hopped up on the rail, ran along it and plopped down into the green pocket.

All perfectly legal, of course. Perhaps that was the weirdest thing about it. If the ball had fallen on the floor, it would have been a foul shot; so, too, if it had stopped and remained up on the rail. As it turned out, it was worth five of the jammiest points ever seen in the history of the game.

On the subject of scoring, what would you have done when the object ball – the black – split in half when struck by the cue ball and the two halves then wheeled away and went into different pockets? Is that worth 14, do you think? Suppose only one half had rolled into a pocket. Would you have given it 3½? (It's a hard life, being a referee; see also page 58.)

HAIR ON THE BALL?

I was playing a match at the Metal Box Company in Vanderbijlpark, South Africa, when I noticed a hair on the cue ball. The referee gave the ball a wipe, and we resumed play. But not only was the hair still present, it had been joined by a second one. We had a closer look, and saw there were two hairline cracks running in opposite directions. Naturally the cracked ball could not be expected to play true, so we put it on the yellow spot and used the yellow ball as the white. Far from feeling put out, I scored 147 using the yellow – the seventh maximum of my career and certainly the most unusual.

Er, foul stroke...er, 3½ away?

SNOOKER IN THE STREET

In the UK Championship a couple of years ago Alex Higgins hit a ball with his usual vigour. But instead of doing the decent thing and staying on the table, this ball wanted to be different. It hit the metal band at the back of the pocket, leapt up in the air – clean off the table – landed on the carpeted floor and kept on rolling. It rolled to the top of a flight of steps, tipped itself over the edge and started to make its way down them.

After an initial hiss of astonishment, the audience watched and waited goggle-eyed, staring at the point where the ball had vanished from view. It was almost as if they expected to see it come rolling back the way it had come, like a movie film in reverse, maybe even jump back on the table.

It'll be back in a minute, he put a reverse screw on it!

But the ball continued merrily on its way, clearly audible. Bomp – bomp – bomp – bomp. Down the stairs it went. Bomp – bomp – bomp . . .

It would be pleasant to record that the ball evaded all attempts to capture it, bounced through the main door and went for a jog in the street outside, halting traffic for half an hour before it hopped on board a bus and disappeared for ever. Unfortunately, someone had the presence of mind to shut the main door of the hall, and the ball was arrested as it approached the threshold and taken in for questioning. Being a generally anti-social ball, it refused to make a statement or give a sample, and is still helping police with their inquiries.

THE ART OF FLUKING

It is not my style to get many flukes (scoring shots that happen unintentionally). Not because I disapprove of them – in snooker you would be daft not to want all the luck that is going – but because generally I do not hit the ball particularly hard and so am less likely to set up as many chance deflections as a player who attacks the ball as though he has just come in from karate lessons.

Flukes, for all that, can be matchwinners. And while it is almost true to say that whenever I score with a fluke shot, a star appears in the East, there was one occasion when a lucky shot with the pink ball made all the difference between winning and losing a championship.

It was 1950, and I was facing John Ford in the final of the amateur championship of Wales. Ford was defending his title, and a few months previously had beaten me all ends up with a style of play I had not encountered before. After that defeat I went home and taught myself the stun and screw game so that I would be a better match for him next time. In the final I was leading 4–3, having performed a great deal better than in our previous match, when I fluked the pink and won the match. I played the pink towards the top pocket; it missed, but came back and dropped into a middle pocket.

Was it a just reward for all my efforts? I think the answer must be no, because flukes are really a matter of chance – and very hard on the opponent as well. What I can say, though, is that I am sure I would not have won the match without that fluke. My opponent had much more experience, and at that stage of the match he was playing the better snooker. He had started slowly – and after the match admitted he had set out thinking I was a pushover. But I had been doing my homework, and sneaked in to take the lead. Then, at 3–1 down, he pulled his game together and began overhauling me. It was a bit like a long-distance race. Just before we reached 1500 metres I still had my nose in front, and thanks to the fluke I was able to keep it there and win. But if the race had been over two miles, he would have won.

LOSING MY MARBLES

I like to think of them as isolated lapses in concentration (whatever anyone else may think). All the same, the memory of two particular incidents still makes the hair stand up on the back of my neck.

The first was when I potted two reds in a row. Not two with the same shot, but with two shots. It was total lunacy – or proof at least of what happens when you let your concentration drop for even a millisecond.

I potted the first red then looked round the table, forming a plan. 'That one there. That colour there,' I said to myself. 'That one over there could cause a bit of trouble . . .' When I had got the whole thing straight in my head, I settled down to play again – and instead of playing a colour I potted a second red!

On the second occasion I was playing John Spencer, who committed a foul shot. The referee awarded me a free ball.

'Thank you,' I said, and looked around the table. What should I do? I could make him play again if I wanted. No, I thought, I'll snooker him. Yes, that'll get him in a lot of trouble. I played the cue ball up behind the yellow.

'Foul shot,' said the referee.

'What? What do you mean?' I said. I looked at John. 'Is he trying to be funny?' I asked.

John did not try to explain; he merely gestured at the table. So I looked again. Foul shot? The white up behind the yellow? Yes. It was beginning to dawn. You may not snooker behind a nominated free ball, except when only the pink and the black remain. It is a rule of the game. I had only been perfectly aware of this rule for about forty years.

'Oh, no-ooo,' I said. 'Dear, oh dear.'

I couldn't say much more, as the match was being televised. Suffice to say, that lapse, mental block, quick trip round the bend, whatever, cost me the game.

THE LONG REST

John Pulman and I were in a doubles match in Birmingham. Each side had played a few safety shots each, and then John had an easy chance of potting a red up in the top right-hand pocket. But to do so, he had to get out the long tackle.

John put his cue on the right-hand side of the table under the cushion, between the yellow and middle pockets. He settled down to play, using the long rest, and potted the red. Then he had to lift the long rest out of the way because the white ball was coming back at him. He got the long tackle up in the air, but then rather unexpectedly the white ball hit a red and was deflected sideways and began to make its way towards John's cue which he had parked down by the side pocket.

There was still time to clear the way, so John quickly transferred the long rest to his left hand, keeping it well up in the air, and reached across with his right hand to pick up his cue. The trouble was, the cue was tucked a little way under the cushion and he could not immediately get hold of it to lift it clear. What should he do?

John promptly found an answer. Roll it out. He took hold of the bottom of the cue, gave it a flick and set it rolling across the table. It was a commendable move to make, in the circumstances, but it had one drawback: by rolling the cue out he sacrificed his control over it.

Before he could grab it again, the runaway cue had rolled all the way across the table – and taken with it all the balls that lay in its path. When the cue came to a halt, the state of play showed about ten balls lying tight up against the left-hand cushion, pinned there by the runaway cue.

It was so completely crazy, John could do little more than put down the long rest, bury his head in his hands and flop on the table. There was no way the referee was going to be able to put all the hijacked balls back in their original positions. We started the game again.

'WE'LL TAKE GOOD CARE OF YOU...'

Well, no, it isn't a billiard ball this time is it, Archie?

I cannot close a chapter entitled 'Oddballs' without recalling Archie, and what happened to him the day he put the billiard ball in his mouth. Archie was a little bit simple, and when four boys in Tredegar – including me – bet him sixpence that he could not put a billiard ball in his mouth, he was only too keen to show us that it could be done. In went the billiard ball, and Archie had earned his sixpence.

Now the problem was to get the billiard ball *out*. To win the bet, Archie had forced the ball in past his teeth, but then could find no way of reversing the process. Archie's teeth and the billiard ball seemed to be clamped to each other semi-permanently. Nothing we could think of would extricate the ball, so we took Archie to the hospital.

We were worried about the strange noises Archie made as part of his attempts to breathe. We also felt a little guilty, no doubt, about setting him up in this predicament. So instead of taking him by the direct route through the town, risking embarrassment and censure, we led Archie round through the park. It took a good while longer, but we delivered him safely (despite his terrible gurgles and bluish complexion).

At the hospital, enough of Archie's front teeth were removed to free the ball. He claimed his sixpence (or 'ficpenf' as he now pronounced it), and the four of us paid out three-halfpence each.

No, I do not recommend that you try it, even in front of a mirror. Billiard balls are surprisingly large, and very hard. You'd be far better off with a grapefruit.

SEX AND THE SNOOKER PLAYER

The partnership between snooker and television may have been a dazzling success on a commercial level, but it is still in the Stone Age as far as sexual opportunity is concerned. At present the rule seems to be: the men do the playing, and the women do the watching.

Chalk your cue for you, sweetie?

PLAYERS ONLY

41

That doesn't seem a very fair or fruitful share-out, does it? Consider, for instance, the male spectator, sat in front of his television set with a six-pack on the carpet beside him. He'd like nothing better than to see a few nicely proportioned ladies bending over the green cloth with their cues poised for action. Why should his missus have all the fun, he wonders, ogling people like Steve Davis, Kirk Stevens, Bill Werbeniuk, to her heart's content? Undoubtedly, the man has a case. Where, then, are the women players?

Some readers may be surprised to learn that, as an organized body, women snooker players have been around longer than television itself. When Ruth Harrison won the first women's professional snooker championship in 1934, television had barely

struggled into existence and was far from being the ideal medium for showing anything as fast-moving as a snooker ball. And although the last professional championship for women was staged in 1950, the signs are that women's snooker is beginning to enjoy a flourishing existence alongside the men's game. The £2000 prize money won by Vera Selby, women's world open champion in 1981, would not set the average male pro twitching with envy, but it was a record payout at the time and we can only assume that the sums available to women players will get larger in the next few years.

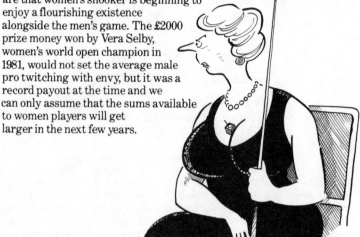

It will then be very interesting to see whether women's snooker really takes off commercially as, for example, women's golf has done. I am not sure that it will. There are certain interesting similarities between snooker and golf, and one crucial difference. Both games look good on television, and another important common factor is that both games require physical power at the highest level of performance. No matter how well a golfer plays a tee shot, if he or she does not hit the ball hard enough it will not go as far as it ought to. The same thing applies to snooker, which in some respects *is* a power game. The table is large, the hitting instrument rather fine, and while timing is an art available to all, the power needed to play the deep screw shots effectively – and keep playing them through a match – is something that few women have mastered.

In golf there is a neat solution to the basic power problem. Move the ladies' tee forward. But in snooker there are no such get-outs. Tinkering with the size of the table would be about as sensible as shrinking tennis courts – and would give the death-blow to mixed doubles, a version of snooker that I feel is ripe for exploitation rather than extinction.

vely cue
:ion...

There are one or two other limiting factors affecting the women's game. Some books on snooker choose to ignore them, but in a bedside book such as this I feel they can be mentioned without stammer or blush. I refer, of course, to big breasts.

No, no, no! I said flatter bra and built-up heels!

Women who have them are among the first to acknowledge that they are not easy to get away from. At a ladies' snooker clinic in Wales, I was approached by an outsized lady who said, with appealing frankness:

'Just look at them. You've got to help me.'

The essence of her problem was that, ideally, the cue needed to pass between her size 44s as she played her shots, but all too often it became jammed. We considered her predicament with suitable gravity. I could sense that she had not signed up for a week-long clinic to hear some flat-chested male offer to hold her bosoms apart while she played. Some longer-lasting solution was called for. I looked her up and down carefully, which did not take much time because her other main characteristic was that she was definitely on the short side.

Lack of height, in fact, was contributing just as much to her snooker problems as the frontal overhang. I noticed that she was wearing flat shoes and suggested that she might do better if she played in high heels – not great spiky stilettoes but shoes with a solid block heel which raised her up maybe a couple of inches.

I did not think she would do anything very rapidly about it. After all, she was away on holiday for a week and would not have bargained on going out and investing in a new pair of shoes to wear for playing snooker. But that is exactly what she did. Next day, there she was, sporting exactly the kind of high heels I had prescribed for her. I was amazed, and full of admiration for her sheer determination to improve her game. She was never going to be a great player, but she was firmly set on being better than she was.

So we had another lesson, and the new shoes *did* make a difference. Wearing them allowed her to be more elevated above the cue instead of right down low, where she had been playing too flat and getting the cue all tangled up. We altered her bridge hand to suit her new posture, and she finished the week a new woman.

LATE NIGHT AT THE OFFICE

Although lots of women are taking up the game nowadays, and having a go themselves instead of just watching the men perform on television and at the clubs, it is still hard to escape from that stereotype of stereotypes – the ordinary male club player who just can't get enough of it (snooker, that is).

There is a story that sums it all up. It is about the boss of a company and his delicious new secretary who has been working for him for just a couple of weeks. One day at the office the work keeps piling up and up; problem follows problem, and the boss and his secretary are worked off their feet holding meetings, taking notes, answering the phone and rushing out urgent letters to clients. At about 2.30 she dashes out to the shops and gets them each a sandwich, and then they plunge back to work. They carry on at their desks until nearly seven o'clock, then the boss decides to call it a day. In gratitude for her help, he offers to drive his secretary back to her flat. When they arrive, she asks him in for a drink. While they are unwinding pleasantly from their hectic day, they remember that they have hardly eaten anything since breakfast.

The secretary offers to run up a quick meal and the boss very readily agrees. He goes out to buy a bottle of wine, comes back, and they enjoy a delightful supper together. Things get better and better between them, and they finish the evening in bed. After such a long and tiring day it is not surprising that they should drop off to sleep. It is after three o'clock in the morning when the boss wakes up and looks at his watch. He hurtles out of bed, and starts pulling on his clothes.

'Quick,' he says to his secretary, as he fumbles with his tie, 'get some whisky and rub it in my hair. Then dust me down with some of this billiard chalk.'

The boss arrives home to be greeted by a middle-class version of the rolling-pin reception. But this time he has an explanation ready for his angry wife.

'I'll tell you exactly what happened,' he says calmly. 'My secretary and I worked late, so I gave her a lift home. She asked me in for a drink and we finished up in bed.'

'Don't you give me that rubbish!' screams the wife. 'You stink of whisky and you're covered in chalk. You've been down that appalling club with your friends playing snooker.'

CHAMPAGNE CHARLIE

People could always tell the serious snooker player in the South Wales coal mines where I was employed. I went to work underground wearing a pair of white canvas gloves. They showed up well in the dark, and if coal mines had been billiards halls they might have given me a certain air of authority, like a kind of foreman-referee. As it happened, neither Ty Trist nor Pochin Colliery remotely resembled a billiards hall. There had to be another explanation.

The real reason for my dandefied mining gear was, quite simply, that I was trying to look after my hands and keep them as clean as possible. No snooker player who wants to get anywhere in the game would seriously think of turning up to play with blackened fingernails and hands engrained either with coal dust or any other kind of dirt.

I saw that...Reardon!

Our sport has a bow-tie image. It is a little old-fashioned, perhaps, but I see no harm in that. The games of billiards and snooker have themselves changed little since the Victorian age, and if you look back at the old engravings – say of the first billiards championship, played in 1870 before the Prince of Wales between John Roberts Senior and William Cook Junior – the players' dress is very similar to what you see on television today. A trifle more sober-looking, I would agree, but the essentials of collar and tie, smartly pressed shirt, dark waistcoat and trousers and well-polished shoes are much the same.

It is an after-dinner image, and it was perfected in the great country houses of more than a century ago, when billiards (and smoking and drinking) were such an indispensable part of gentlemanly behaviour that they had their own specially designed rooms to which the gentlemen retired after dinner. Once out of sight of the ladies, they could safely remove their jackets and, lo and behold! Underneath they were dressed like snooker players.

THE SHIRT OFF HIS BACK

Against such an impressive historic background, no wonder I felt horrified by the prospect of appearing improperly attired at the very smart Eccentric Club in London. I was due to play there before a dinner-jacketed audience, and had arrived in good time for my appearance only to find, after unpacking in my room in the club, that I had forgotten to put in a dress shirt. Calamity! The shops were shut and there was no chance of buying or hiring a replacement.

I went down to the foyer of the club to see if a miracle could be conjured up. It was also better than remaining alone in my room cursing and banging my head on the wall.

The miracle duly appeared. His name was Bruce Stevans, and he was an Australian bank manager I had met in Melbourne. I was naturally glad to see him, especially when he was so far from home, but he did not quite realize just *how* glad I was to see him until I began to show an almost indecent interest in the immaculate dress shirt which he was intending to wear at my snooker evening.

'That's a nice shirt,' I said. 'Did you bring it with you?'

'No,' he said. 'I just hired it this afternoon.'

'Oh,' I said. 'Well, it's very nice anyway. Tell me, what size collar do you take?'

'Sixteen and a half,' he replied.

'That's amazing!' I said. 'I take sixteen and a half.'

'Oh, really,' he said, politely.

'Yes,' I said. 'But I've left mine at home and I want to borrow yours.'

When he finally got my message, he allowed himself a moment or two for proper bank managerial reflection, then generously agreed, settling for one of my plain white shirts while I hastily pulled on the frilly job appropriate to my station as an incurable exhibitionist.

SOCKERAMA

I was playing at a Pontin's camp, at Barton Hall in Devon. After a late night I rose in a bit of a hurry, shaved, dressed, combed the hair, and minutes later I was in the snooker room. I did my usual stuff, and at the end I was following the people out when a young lady came up to me.

'That was a very nice show,' she said, 'I enjoyed that. But tell me', she added, 'did you know that your socks don't match?'

I looked down. It was true. The right sock was a different colour from the left. Trying not to sound as silly as I felt, I said to the young lady:

'Ah, yes. And I've got another pair like this at home!'

WHEN IS A TIE NOT A TIE?

Snooker outfits are a bit brighter than in the Joe Davis years, when black mohair was the rule for suits, and ties were bought at the same shop that undertakers go to for their gear. Nowadays there are players who forsake ties altogether.

At first the 'Kirk Stevens' open-neck look was frowned on, but I think most people will be prepared to move with the times so long as the player dresses neatly and presents himself well when he is in the public eye. To my mind, where the image slips is when the player puts on a tie in the changing room, comes out front looking immaculate – and then wrecks the impression he has made by tearing off the tie before he begins to play.

Recently our Association has cracked down by insisting that a player must produce a doctor's certificate stating that he has an allergy, or whatever, that makes it painful for him to wear a tie. What is more, the player must produce a new certificate for every tournament at which he proposes not to wear a tie. So it will be no good just waving the same old tattered bit of paper, pretending it is some kind of magic passport to undress.

Talking of paper reminds me, for some strange reason, of money. And, indeed, a time may come when it will actually pay players to wear certain clothes. At the moment the clothing manufacturers have not managed to find a way into snooker, which is not like other sports – tennis, say, or soccer – where you can design a logo and fix it on the players' outfits. Where, for instance, would you put the logo on a snooker player's shirt so that it would actually be seen – not just when the player wears that brand of shirt but also when ordinary members of the public buy them? That type of sponsorship does not seem to work for snooker as it does for other sports where the outfits are designed mainly for outdoor use and are generally more basic, i.e. a shirt, shorts and socks. In snooker we wear layers of *indoor* clothing, and when we finish playing we naturally put on a jacket, thereby hiding the parts that could be earning money for us! It's tragic, really.

It's not just the sponsorship – he even has a note excusing him from wearing trousers.

I was sponsored for a while by Marsden's, a firm of tailors in Stoke-on-Trent. That was great fun, because they provided me with a set of nine brightly coloured jackets, and I wore a new one every evening so that the crowd were always kept guessing about what I would turn up in next. As my finale, I arrived on the last evening in full Champagne Charlie rig with a top hat and a cape, covering a brilliant jacket in scarlet silk. Unfortunately, some grateful member of the

public decided I looked like Count Dracula, and it took several months to live down the notion that I actually sank my teeth into my opponents' necks. That's not my method at all. And I'm not telling you what is!

SNOOKER

TONIGHT

VERSUS

RAY REARDON

(18)

NO CHILDREN UNDER 18 ADMITTED

'FOR THOSE OF YOU WITH BLACK AND WHITE BALLS...'

When it began, it was just as bad for the TV people as it was for us. The technical difficulties of bringing snooker to the screen were considerable. Positions for all the lights and four or five cameras had to be worked out, also the best place for the commentator to sit so he could speak to the television audience without interrupting the players' concentration.

Shhh!

Nowadays it is rare for a player to be able to pick up the commentator's remarks. With fourteen years' experience behind them, the BBC have got their transmissions down to a fine art. It is a far cry from the début of *Pot Black* in 1969, when 'Whispering' Ted Lowe had to breathe his comments into a mouth-mike from a position in the audience about fifteen feet from the table.

Imagine the commentator murmuring away in his best soft-voiced churchwarden style: '. . . now he's aiming to put the red into the middle pocket. This will give him a good position on the black. He can take the black to the left-hand black pocket then bring the cue ball back and put the red in the opposite black pocket . . .'

I turn round. I have heard all this quite distinctly – and it's a lot of nonsense. I'm not **'Oh no he isn't!'** going to do that at all. I look up to make

'Oh yes he is!'

sure the camera is not on me. Then I point down for the commentator's benefit at the red I intend to play.

'... on the other hand, he does have an alternative shot,' whispers the commentator immediately. 'He *may* try for the other red into the middle pocket.' So *that's* how we used to do it. The magic of television!

It would not be right to reminisce about our primitive days on television without mentioning an earlier sport that for sheer suspense can have had few equals. Radio snooker. This was a real audience-gripper. Live before the listening audience, the players played, the commentator commentated and – most exciting of all – every half minute or so people in lounges and bedrooms throughout the country heard the dramatic click of the balls.

I am not truly surprised that radio snooker had only a short career. It had to be presented live, and if nothing much was happening on the table, there was little the commentator could do about it. The announcement 'He's played a safety shot' would be followed by a description of the position of the balls, which in those days would have been as clear as mud to most listeners. This would be followed by a description of the next piece of play: 'Now his opponent has played a safety shot.' Good stuff, eh?

FRED IN A FIX

By the time the televised highlights of a tournament are shown in the evening, the commentator's more blatant gaffes have usually been edited out, though some of them may be lovingly stored, set to music and shown in one of those sets of funny clips which are so popular.

Good grief! Most players just sit quietly between shots and wait their turn...

One such moment occurred when Fred Davis was playing. The white ball had finished in a very awkward position. Fred walked all round the table trying to find the best way to get at it. He stood on his right leg; no good. He stood on his left leg; no good. He leaned far out over the table; still he could not get at the cue ball. He tried to bring one knee up on top of the table to improve his leverage. Watching his struggles, the commentator murmured:

'Well, there's Fred, now aged sixty-seven, and he's having a bit of difficulty getting his leg over.'

Then Fred took hold of his knee and tried to give it a push-up.

'Never mind,' added the commentator. 'Now he's using his left hand as well!'

GAME FOR A LAUGH

We have had a lot of fun over the years with John Smythe, one of our regular referees. It is his own fault, really, but John has one of those infectious and uncontrollable laughs. Once we got him started, he had great difficulty in stopping himself. Obviously, the best place to get him going was when we were live on TV.

There was one story which tickled him so much, it was cruel to remind him of it as often as we did. The story was about a man whose greatest ambition was to shoot a bear. He went out to Canada on holiday, bought a rifle, drove out to a game park and set off on foot in search of a bear. After a short while he spotted one, up on a hill. Excited, he ran back to his car, got his rifle, shot the bear, then ran back to the car again and put the rifle out of sight.

His next problem was to get the bear back down to the car. The bear was huge and very heavy, and the hunter's only solution seemed to be to sling it across his back and drag it along. So he put the bear's left front paw over his left shoulder, its right front paw over his right shoulder, slid the animal across his back as best he could, then started to ease his way forward.

The going was slow and hard, and the man was so engrossed by what he was doing that he did not hear the game warden coming.

'Aha!' cried the game warden, jumping across in front of him, and waving a pistol. 'So you're the man who's been shooting our bears. I've caught you red-handed. You're in big trouble.'

'What? What do you mean?' asked the man.

'Come on,' said the game warden, 'you've just killed a bear, and I've caught you.'

'Bear?' said the man. 'What bear? What are you talking about?'

'That bear on your back.'

The man turned his head in mock astonishment, and pretended he was seeing the bear for the first time. 'Aaah!' he cried, looking up at the great heavy corpse on his back. 'Get off! Get off!' He began brushing himself with frantic strokes. 'Get off! Filthy bear!'

It was a fairly silly joke, but every time John Smythe heard it he burst into one of his uncontrollable fits of laughter. Just a quick reference would do. A bit of frantic shoulder-brushing was enough to get John in the mood. Then, in front of the television cameras, one of the players would ask him a question. It was like getting a schoolboy to speak when his mouth was full of sweets which should not be there. Up went John's hand to his mouth. 'Pffff!' It was all great television – especially if you knew what was going on.

Another chance to get at the referee on television is at the start of a *Pot Black* match, when you have tossed a coin to decide the order of play and the referee has to announce the result.

He stands between the two players rehearsing his big line, which might be, for example: 'Mr Spencer has won the toss and will break.'

The players have other ideas. They set up a whispering campaign, telling him: 'Mr Spencer has won the break and will toss. Mr Spencer has won the break and will toss.'

'Shut up, shut up,' mutters the referee. 'It's "Mr Spencer has won the toss and will break".'

At last the sign comes from the Floor Manager. 'You're on.' The referee raises his head smartly and snaps out:

'Mr Spencer has won the toss and will break.'

Or so he thinks. But what actually comes out is:

'Mr Spencer has won the break and will toss.'

As soon as the words are out, the referee *knows* what he has said. 'Grrrr!' he screams, tearing out fistfuls of hair. 'Cut! Cut!' calls the exasperated director. Chaos all round. Lovely.

STRIKE ME PINK

It's simple, you daft wossock! When he's potted the light grey ball he goes on to the mid grey one and then the dark grey. On the other hand, he may decide...

55

The real success story of snooker on television can be counted from the advent in 1974 of colour television. This had a number of benefits. Colour made snooker more accessible as a sport and as a spectacle to thousands of people who had never played it in their lives. The proportion of women viewers has risen remarkably, from about 10 or 15 per cent in those days to something approaching 40 per cent in the last two or three years.

There were bound to be a few commentators' gaffes, especially during the changeover period when the older black and white sets were still as common as colour sets. These gaffes cropped up in virtually every sport (except perhaps cricket), and in snooker the most famous remark was made by the commentator who solemnly said:

'For those of you with black and white sets, the blue ball is next to the yellow.'

BANG! BANG!

One of snooker's most extraordinary moments on television came during a recent Embassy tournament. Ted Lowe was commentating as usual, when his director issued a brisk instruction in his ear:

'Finish your sentence and then we're going to stop.'

Ted was still wondering what on earth was going on when all his monitors went blank. He had sound contact, though, and the next thing he heard was an almighty 'Bang!'

He had no idea what was happening. Then it was explained to him that BBC television had switched suddenly to

The things some people will do when they can't get a ticket!

56

Kensington to show the SAS blasting their way into the Iranian
Embassy to end the siege there. A few moments later, the newsflash
was over and Ted was told to stand by again with his commentary.
Within seconds he was back on the air, making the
once-in-a-lifetime comment:

'And now, from one Embassy to another Embassy.'

THANK YOU, FANS

It is wonderful, through television, to have such large numbers of keen
followers of the game, and many of them are pretty knowledgeable, not
just about the basic rules, the values of the different colours and the
order in which they are played, but about some of the less familiar laws
as well. If I have any reservations about television, it is that it has made
the game look too easy.

On a television screen a full-sized snooker table
looks like a toy. Consequently, some people find it hard to understand
why we pros do not pot everything in sight all the time. They (the
audience) can see what needs to be done – red in there, come back for
the black, etc – and sometimes they seem to wonder just what is holding
us back. Snooker, to some, is almost entirely a matter of getting balls in
pockets. This is not wholly their fault in that air time is limited, and a
programme of highlights will show comparatively little of the early
phases of a frame, where safety shots and sound defensive play are
more to be admired than wild aggression – which is invariably a sign
that the player has lost his nerve or does not know what he is doing.

However, safety shots don't rack up the points, so
some spectators do get a bit disgruntled for what I would say were not
the best of reasons. At the same time, we players have to remember that
we would not be where we are if there were not a vast army of
enthusiastic fans out there.

Whether the public should actually own you as well is
something I have mixed feelings about. At any rate, the punters are
entitled to their opinions, however eccentric, and if someone comes up
to me after a game and wants to tell me something, I do my best to
listen.

'You should have won' is an accusation I have learned
to live with, and in fact I have a fixed response. I agree with them.
'You're quite right,' I say. 'I should have won. I can
see you are very knowledgeable about the game.' Unfortunately it is
usually necessary to add: 'Now, I haven't eaten for eight hours, so if you
wouldn't mind taking that autograph book out of my steak and kidney
pie . . .'

WELL PLAYED, THE REF

Who would want to be a referee? It must be worse than being a head waiter. When there are flies in the soup, or the soup doesn't come, or the table is in the wrong place, or there is a funny smell – then everyone wants to tear a strip off the head waiter. But when everything runs perfectly, no-one notices if he's even clocked on.

That is what you *might* think about snooker referees. But the truth is more complicated. To start with, you have to make allowance for the fact that, for better or for worse, a snooker referee *is* noticed. He is *on television*. Whether a match is smooth-running or controversial, his missus can see him, and so can the neighbours. He is a presence, and he has a suit to go with it. White gloves and all. As he steps briskly round the table, various measuring devices can be heard making important clicking noises in his pockets. What is more, he has a special cloth for polishing the balls, to divest them of chalk. And at major tournaments, he is wired up for sound.

His voice is the Voice of Authority. And doesn't everybody love it when Authority makes a bloomer? I'll give you an example. Two days before writing this, I was in a tight corner during a match. All I could do was roll the cue ball along the rail and touch the red. As I got down, I noticed the referee peering intently at the red. 'Hullo,' I thought. 'He'll be after me if I miss it.'

I played the shot. The cue ball rolled gently up the table and just tickled the red, enough to move it about half an inch. Exactly what I wanted. I nodded to myself and straightened up.

'Foul!'

I stared at him in disbelief. Were we in the same game? Fortunately, it turned out that we were, because in the next instant the referee corrected the call. What made me smile about the incident, though, was the way the referee had not been able to stop himself in the first place. He had been itching so badly to call the foul, he was already over the edge before the cue ball had stopped.

It's bound to happen, I suppose, when people have to concentrate for such long periods of time. The main thing is that we all try to keep our sense of humour when things go a little astray. If we were all a lot of misery-gobs at the table – players and referees – I am quite sure that people would not want to watch the game as much as they do. The fact that we manage to smile after a bad shot, or after losing a match, must work in the game's favour.

Like all sports, especially those with big-money prizes, the players and officials need to enjoy what they are doing. As soon as it becomes too much of a business, it ceases to be a sport. And while it is possible to understand *why* some players in other sports get so heated, even violent, on the field of play – especially in team sports, though one-against-one sports are not exempt from this – it is impossible to condone that kind of conduct. I am equally certain that there can be no room, ever, for that sort of nonsense in snooker. Any

'F-f-f-f...'
'Wait for it, ref!'

referee who is reading this can rest assured: the day players start jabbing each other in the eye with their cues, or hair-pulling, or even putting the knee in as they cross paths at the table . . . the day that happens, I shall be off. This dog is too old for such tricks.

And now it looks as if a little bit of needle is creeping in...

THE CRUNCH

I was recently asked where snooker referees come from. There is no easy answer to that question. At some levels of the game you find referees where I feel there is really no need for them; the players ought to be able to sort things out between them. The crunch comes at professional tournaments, where, with ever-mounting prize money at stake, an experienced adjudicator is essential. But who should he be? Logically, the choice points to a former professional player. However, I am not convinced that the referees should be professional themselves.

The fact that they, as well as the players, rely on snooker for their living puts a certain invidious pressure on them to conform, and maybe avoid making an unpopular decision. A controversial verdict over something that is really hard to pin down – a deliberate miss shot, for instance – could provoke a huge row later, and could result in that referee never being asked to officiate at another tournament. If that happened, he would lose his livelihood. This is a very delicate area at present, and I am not sure we have all the answers.

TOOLS OF THE TRADE

We have been able to defuse some potentially explosive areas thanks to a machine. At one time it was simply one man's eyes that determined whether a ball would spot or not. If the referee got it wrong, it was highly exasperating for the players since it often affected their entire strategy for the frame. Now, there's a device that takes the pain out of spotting. It's a little marker, half the diameter of a ball, which the referee places on the table facing the object ball, and moves towards it. If the marker stands up, without touching the object ball, the ball will spot; if it does not, the ball won't spot.

In addition, the referee also carries a semi-circular device in glass or heavy plastic which is designed to fit exactly round a snooker ball. This is to mark the ball's position before it is removed from the table, for polishing if it's got chalk on, or a hair, or to inspect it for damage. Ah, the wonders of technology. One day, I expect the referee himself will be made of plastic and glass. That wouldn't be so bad; at least, if he was a robot, we wouldn't have to buy him drinks afterwards!

THE PINK THAT GOT AWAY

When *Pot Black* was being planned, in 1969, it was obvious from the start that a referee would be an important part of the presentation. For the first series, the man chosen was a famous old professional player, Sydney Lee. Dear old Sydney had been at his peak in the Thirties, and is better remembered as a billiards player than for his feats at the snooker table. However, he was a popular choice, and when the day dawned to start filming, there was Sydney.

In one physical aspect Sydney was outstanding. He had enormous feet. They were big enough for walking across water; unfortunately, they played him up a lot, and because of this he had a funny, rather lopsided way of going about. On this particular occasion, though, it was not so much Sydney's feet that caused the problem, as his hands.

To mark his selection as referee for the pioneering television series, Sydney had gone out and bought himself a new pair of white gloves. Not just the ordinary cotton gloves, such as referees usually wear because they give a good grip on balls which are inclined to be slippery – oh no. Sydney bought himself a wonderful pair of white *silk* gloves.

Filming began, and after a few minutes someone potted the pink. Sydney picked it out and went to re-spot it. This was trickier than usual, because the pink spot was surrounded by a cluster of reds. There was just room to put the ball back in position, provided it was lowered in carefully from above.

Sydney gripped the top quarter of the ball as firmly as he could in his silk-gloved fingers. His hand craned out over the pink spot and he began to lower the ball. Lower . . . lower, and . . . ooops! Still some inches from its intended resting place, the pink ball spurted from Sydney's not very tight silky grasp and bombed down on the table, striking several of the surrounding reds.

As inevitably as ripples follow a stone landing in water, so the reds began rippling outwards across the table. Sydney's reaction was instinctive.

'Oooh!' he cried, and lunged forwards on his dodgy feet to cradle the escaping balls in his arms and bring them back together again.

It was a brave gesture, but doomed. There was no way Sydney was going to be able to replace all those reds in their original positions. They had to start the game again. It's a wonder, really, they didn't rename the TV series there and then. How about *Spot Pink*? Or *Drop Pink*?

MORE TROUBLE WITH THE PINK

The pink ball was the focal point of a nightmarish experience involving another referee. Alex Higgins was playing Steve Davis. Steve potted the pink ball and it was clear to the referee, while the pink was still on the runners under the middle pocket, that he would have problems re-spotting it.

While this was going through his mind, the referee walked round the table intending to pick up the pink ball with his left hand. But instead, through some inexplicable mental block, he reached out with his right hand and picked up the white ball from the table. He went to try and re-spot this ball, thinking it was the pink. Then he looked down at his hand, and saw that he was holding the white.

Blank horror was written all over his face. What was this? How did that get there? Higgins shot out of his seat and dashed over to look. He was glaring at the white ball in the referee's hand, and the referee was glaring round the room wondering who he could blame for his extraordinary mistake.

Everyone else thought it was hilarious, of course. And there was still more joy to come as the embarrassed referee tried to gather his wits together and remember where the white ball had been lying before he had so mysteriously grabbed it. Was it there? Over there? Back there a bit? Why don't they stop laughing? Why don't the floorboards just open up and swallow me?

THE EYE OF THE BEHOLDER

The newspapers inflated the incident out of proportion. I *did* have a disagreement not so long ago with my friend John Smythe, but I recall it here to show, once again, that if you retain your sense of humour you are more than halfway to winning the battle.

At the UK tournament I was playing Jimmy White. Jimmy missed the ball, and John Smythe awarded a free ball. Jimmy wanted to dispute the decision, but I got up from my seat and persuaded him to calm down while I had a look. The way I saw it, Jimmy was right. It was not a free ball. And if I got a free ball in that position, I would win the frame. So I said to John Smythe that I was sure it wasn't a free ball, and would he mind taking another look. But John was adamant:

'My eyes tell me it's a free ball.'

There was no arguing with that. Instead, to nullify the decision, I asked Jimmy to play again. Then, a little while later, I was in play when John Smythe suddenly called:

'Touching balls.'

No way were those balls touching. There was a clear gap between them. I said as much, and John replied:

'My eyes tell me those balls are touching.'

I had to play a different shot. Afterwards, in the dressing-room,

Which touching balls?
Which table for a start?

I said to John: 'Look. You have given two wrong decisions out there today. I've no personal axe to grind, because one was in my favour and one was not. But, for your own good, I think you ought to have your eyes tested.'

I also told him that in half an hour I had an interview with David Vine who wanted to ask me about the controversial decisions. I said that I was going to tell him exactly what I thought – even though I would be tactful about it. And that was what happened. I explained at some length how difficult it was for referees to please everyone: how they had to administer the game, see everything, keep out of the way of the cameras, not block the view of any one section of the spectators for too long. Turning to the subject of the controversial decisions, I said that John was completely unbiased and a good referee. All the same, if he said that his eyes told him that it was a free ball, and later that the balls were touching... then he ought to have his eyes examined.

They lapped it up. It is everyone's joy to say on television that there is something wrong with a referee's eyesight. The fact that I was doing it for John's own good tended to be overlooked by the sensation-mongers. However, while the press enjoyed itself for a couple of days, John thought about it... and let his sense of humour guide him over what to do next.

A few days later I was playing John Spencer in a snooker evening at the Eccentric Club in London. Who was the referee? John Smythe. We started the game. No incidents. Everything ran smoothly until, after a few frames, the cue ball and a red came to rest quite close together, but still a good two inches apart. John Spencer said:

'Touching balls!'

As the crowd erupted, the effect on John Smythe was electric. He went up to the edge of the table, glared fiercely at the balls for a moment, said nothing, then from an inside pocket he drew out the biggest magnifying glass I have ever seen – a real Sherlock Holmes special – and began to scan the two balls through it. He held it there until the audience's laughter had subsided, then pronounced firmly:

'Not touching!'

Since then, John has gone from strength to strength. He has become a very popular figure on the circuit, and even gets asked to make appearances in his own right. Discerning observers also notice something else: he has taken to wearing spectacles when he referees.

TALES FROM THE CIRCUIT

A keen golfer drove up to his club, eager for a game, but the weather prospects were not promising. The sky was getting darker, the clouds turning from grey to a menacing purple. As he walked across the car park with his golf bag, the first large spots began plopping on the gravel.

HAVE BALLS
WILL TRAVEL

'Doesn't look too good,' thought the golfer, hurrying into the clubhouse. Despite the weather, he decided to see who was around and try and fix up a game. He leant his clubs against the wall and put his head round the door of the bar. It was empty except for a group of three members, two of whom he vaguely recognized, sitting round a table in the corner. At the sound of the door opening, the three members looked up and one of them gave him a wave and called:

'Hello. One for a four?'

'Great,' said the newcomer. 'Yes, I'll be with you in a couple of minutes.'

He walked into the locker-room with a smile on his face. 'That's a bit of luck,' he said to himself as he changed into his wet-weather golfing gear – the rainproof windcheater, shiny trousers, etc. He picked up his golf bag and umbrella and went outside.

Now the rain was zipping down. Blown almost sideways by the wind, and with small but vicious hailstones working like tracer bullets, the downpour soaked the poor chap from top to toe before he could even get his umbrella raised. When at last he managed to force the spokes down the shaft and get it hoisted, he looked around for his playing partners. No-one in sight.

The light in the bar was still on so he went over to the window and looked in. The three members were still sitting round their table, drinking and talking. The lone golfer tapped on the window to attract their attention. When at last they looked up he called:

'Come on, then. One for a four, you said.'

'Yes,' replied one of the indoor members. 'But we're going to play snooker, not golf!'

TRICKY STUFF

Part of the snooker pro's stock-in-trade is his range of trick shots. Quite often we get requests for certain favourite tricks at the end of an exhibition, and we usually try to oblige. By that I mean we are usually happy to perform the trick, even though the end result may not always be what we originally had in mind.

I was at the Pot Black Club in Plymouth one night when somebody called out:

'Do the one with the whisky bottle.'

'Right,' I said, and a whisky bottle was fetched and placed on the table. On top of the bottle I balanced a snooker ball. I prefer a round bottle for this shot, because they are less likely to break if something goes wrong and they fall over. On this occasion the manager had produced a triangular bottle, but it looked about the right size, so I let it be.

The trick is to fire the cue ball at another ball placed about six inches from the bottle. The cue ball then 'jumps' and knocks the 'whisky' ball clean away from the top of the bottle. On that

Show off! Why can't he just unscrew the bottle like anyone else?

particular evening the cue ball took off after impact with the first ball but something was wrong. It failed to gain enough height. It drove into the neck of the triangular whisky bottle and shattered it. Moments later a dark stain of neat Scotch was spreading over the cloth.

After the first few moments of terrible silence I gave out a slightly high-pitched shriek of horror, and the audience helpfully roared their appreciation – the happy witnesses of a four-star disaster – and several club officials dashed into the toilets to search for towels and paper to swab the whisky.

'Hey!' I managed to cry as the officials rushed back. 'Not towels. They'll only draw out the dye. Get a bucket of water. Quick!'

The bucket arrived and I chucked the contents all over the table.

'Always take my Scotch with water,' I said.

Those with an official interest in the state of the table did not laugh. They looked at me as if I was barmy. They could have been right, because at the time I did not know for sure that it would work. I just had a strong feeling that it would have been unwise to try and mop up the whisky with towels since this could only have drained out some of the colour and produced a piebald cloth – which I would have felt bound to replace at a cost of several hundred pounds. As it was, I asked the manager to give the cloth a couple of days to dry out properly. When I telephoned him later to see how it was, he said it was looking a little pale in places but they could live with that.

You may well say I got off lightly. It is not always like that, and hardly ever in Rotherham. They have some hard men in the clubs in Rotherham. At one place, I was finishing the evening with a series of trick shots, and all went well until the last shot, which I missed.

This is bound to happen occasionally. The tricks are not easy to do, and from time to time it is inevitable that some will go wrong. The trouble is, I never know in advance *which* of the tricks in the repertoire is going to cause problems.

In the front row at Rotherham was a little old-fashioned Yorkshireman. He wore a suit with a waistcoat, a cloth cap, and a cigarette hung from his mouth. I went for the trick shot a second time. Again I missed it. The man in the front row cried:

'Come on, Ray, for Christ's sake hurry up and get it. Me pie and peas are getting cold at home.'

IRISH TIMES

Irish people have the essential gift of being funny without, apparently, making any effort. New Irish stories reach me constantly – and I can assure you that not all these stories feature men in wellies and donkey jackets on a building site. To give you an example:

There were two fellers in wellies and donkey jackets in a snooker hall. They had been playing for two hours, concentrating intensely. It was a tight game. Michael versus Sean. Then the steward, who had been watching them, could bear it no longer. He came over and took the triangle off the reds.

It's not fair, is it? No. And it's not fair, either, to tell you about the Irish snooker player who went to the Motor Show, and spent the rest of the day walking round the car park.

Here's another gem from the Emerald Isle. I was over there for a tournament once, and a little lad approached me in my hotel lobby. He was immaculately turned out in a suit with long trousers, a waistcoat, and a neat bow tie. His hair was slicked back. Obviously he was a snooker fan; he was probably aged about six or seven.

'Excuse me, mister,' he said, 'could I have your autograph, please.'

He held out an autograph book and a pen.

'Certainly, son,' I said, and accepted the book and pen. I opened the book and asked him. 'What's your name, son?'

'Patrick,' he said. 'But I want *your* autograph.'

That one's by Ray Reardon, that's by Eddie Charlton, that's by Alex Higgins and...

THE METAL DETECTOR

If further proof were needed that the Irish have a special way of regarding the world, I was staying once with an Irish friend called Des Cameron. He lives just outside Dublin and is a snooker enthusiast and promoter. One evening in his snooker room I could not help noticing a small army of strange objects on poles ranged in one corner against the wall. He had about thirty of them. I asked him what they were.

'They're metal detectors,' he said, with the air of a man who knew exactly what he had in the corner of his snooker room.

'But you've got about thirty of them,' I pointed out.

'Yes, I know,' he said. It was not easy to shake this man. He added: 'I sell them.'

'Oh,' I said, 'you sell them. How much do they cost?'

'Anything,' he said, 'anything between £30 and £250.'

'Well,' I said, doubtfully, 'they all look the same to me.'

And they did. They all seemed to have the same head on them; they were all the same length, all battery-operated.

'No, no, no,' said Des. 'Go in the other room and hide some coins.'

I did as he said. In his lounge I hid three 10p pieces: one under the carpet, one under the pouffe and one under the seat of the settee. It was daft, really. I mean, where in a house can you hide something so that a metal detector won't find it? Anyway, my host was not to be deterred.

At a signal from me, he came into his lounge wearing the full works (the £250 model presumably) with headphones and everything, and started moving slowly up and down with it. 'Dzzzz-dzzzz.' Round the armchair. 'Dzzzz-dzzzz.' Over in the corner he went, like a Hoover with legs. Suddenly he, or it, struck. 'Bip-bip-bip-bip . . .'

Des bent down and snatched up the 10p piece that I had hidden under the carpet. He wrenched off his headphones and punched the air. 'I found one! I found one!'

'Of course you found one,' I said. 'No need to get that pleased about it, is there? You found a piece of metal in your own lounge using your own metal detector. Heavens, in another couple of hours you would have found the other two coins as well. Bound to. What's so marvellous about that?'

'All right, all right,' agreed Des, calming down gradually. 'I tell you what, if it's a nice day tomorrow we'll go down to the beach. You never know what we'll find down there.'

I'd prefer to use the spider really...

Next morning the sun shone and by ten o'clock we were down on the beach. There were two couples out there already, sitting on the beach fairly close together with six or seven children between them.

I was walking behind Des, who, now we were outside, was wearing goggles as well as earphones, and was tracking slowly over the beach with his machine. 'Dzzz-dzzz-dzzz-dzzz.' Usual noise.

I thought to myself: 'What a lovely day it is. And I'm walking along the beach behind this nutter with a machine that's more irritating to listen to than a plague of mosquitoes. I must be crazy. In fact, I must be worse than he is . . .'

We continued our ramble in the 21st century until I felt a tugging at my trouser leg. I looked down. It was a small girl from one of the family groups. She must have been about five or six years old. She said to me:

'What's he looking for?'

I said: 'My dear, he's looking for money.'

'Jasus,' she said, looking over at Des with pity in her eyes. 'He must be poor!'

WORLD TOUR

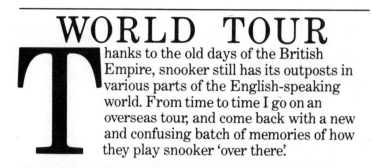

Thanks to the old days of the British Empire, snooker still has its outposts in various parts of the English-speaking world. From time to time I go on an overseas tour, and come back with a new and confusing batch of memories of how they play snooker 'over there'.

       Which country would I be in, for example, if the snooker table looked like a battlefield, littered with the corpses of flies, mosquitoes and gigantic tree-bugs which the referee dealt with by smashing them into the cloth with a rolled-up newspaper? If you have ever been to South Africa, you will naturally understand that these are normal playing conditions. The heat was stifling, too, in that colliery social club near Johannesburg. But the biggest problem was neither the heat nor the table, but the floor.

My hosts had done such a marvellous job smoothing and polishing the floor to the evenness of marble and the brilliance of a diamond . . . that I could hardly stand up on it. After sliding about helplessly for a few minutes, I pointed out the difficulty and my hosts called a halt. I went into the bar while the committee got down to tackling the problem. Five minutes later they said it was all done, all OK.

We went back in. I was expecting them to have laid a piece of matting or carpet on the floor. Instead, they had coated it thickly with white scouring powder. I played on. The problem of keeping a foothold was cured, but only at the cost of creating another: as my opponent and I circled the table, we agitated this Transvaal Vim which then rose up in little clouds around us, crept into our nostrils, sat in our hair, and burned our eyes till we wept. So now we could stand up but we could not see the balls except as dim targets that floated before our eyes like objects in a mirage. If only I had thought of it at the time, we could have borrowed some goggles off the miners!

It was better when they kept falling over!

LOOKING FOR THE WHITE MAN

I was on tour in Madras. With me was Mike Green, Secretary of our Association, who had decided to come out to India for a holiday. We were invited to a reception and soon found ourselves sitting among a sea of black-faced gentlemen while the President of the local Association made a speech of welcome. After several minutes of this I was nodding off nicely when I heard the President say:

'And so, what a great honour it is to have with us today, all the way from United Kingdom, the Secretary of the World Professional Billiards and Snooker Association. Will Mr Michael Green please stand up?'

Since Mike and I were the only two white men in the place, I thought it hilarious that he should be asked to stand up and identify himself. But he, always a true gent, obliged, and received an enthusiastic ovation followed by a huge garland of flowers. This was draped round his neck and covered his entire body down to the hips; there was even an extra dangling bit left over, which hung between his legs with a faintly suggestive air. It was more like being somewhere in the South Seas. I thought of asking him for a dance, but he had a strange look in his eye and might well have accepted.

EVERY ONE A WINNER

While I was in Madras I was invited to the races. I went to a meeting which had eight races; I was guided to a luxury box in the grandstand and went clean through the card. The only slightly odd feature of this betting coup was that I did not myself pick the horses.

I was the guest of a bookmaker, and he marked my card for me. He also instructed me not to place any bets with him, but with a colleague who had been forewarned. Not only that, the other bookmaker would offer me an extra point for every bet I placed. In other words, if the horse's odds were 3–1, he would give me 4–1.

That was good enough for me. I placed my bets in advance and sat back in solitary grandeur in my box. A few yards behind my seat stood a small crowd of people, and after each race they called out to me:

'Hey! hey!'

I turned round.

'Did you back it?'

I smiled and gave them the thumbs-up sign.

'Hurrah!' they all cheered.

I haven't a clue who they were.

Eight times this happened, and my original stake money of five rupees rose to a total of 17,000 rupees. All of which explains the presence in my lounge at home of an ornately carved and decorated table that looks more like a temple than a resting-place for teacups. It is not my usual practice to buy lumps of furniture in exotic places and ferry them 5,000 miles back to North Staffordshire, but, as I found in India, you can't export your winnings unless you do the local economy a favour or two in return.

It's not the gift itself, Sue, it's the thought that counts!

A PRESENT FROM INDIA

INDIA

THE

Never mind what they do on the golf course, Blue, you can't do it here!

ROCK GOLF

In Australia I have played in all kinds of strange venues, out in the bush in mining camps miles from anywhere, whisking all over the place by light plane and helicopter. But for me the oddest playing surfaces were on the golf courses rather than in the billiard halls.

At Wyalla, for instance, which is near Adelaide, the course is so rocky that your ball only has to get an unlucky bounce to go pinging off fifty yards in the wrong direction. As for the greens, it is best to think of them as blacks, because that is their natural colour. They are made of a mixture of coal dust and oil which is refined, dried and pressed, and when you land a golf ball on the 'black' it simply plugs into the dust and stops.

Now you get ready to putt. You are given a T-shaped scraper and with this you are allowed two scrapes to mark out a path to the hole. You mark the ball's position by drawing a V in the dust with the ball at the apex of the V. Then you take the scraper, which is about two feet across, and pull it all the way to the hole. Then you do it again. When you are finally ready to putt, you replace your ball in the apex of the V and whack it down this smooth-bottomed channel you have just cleared away. You have to hit the ball pretty hard, but if you are straight there is a good chance it will go in. Even if you overcompensate and really belt the ball, it rarely travels more than a couple of inches past the hole before it gets clogged in the dust again.

Golf, they call it.

THE SMALLEST BILLIARDS
HALL IN THE WORLD

Back, briefly, to South Africa for a flying glimpse of the smallest exhibition hall I have ever seen. It was on a farm in the wilds of the Orange Free State. When I arrived at the farm after a 200-mile drive from Johannesburg, I asked to see the table on which I was due to demonstrate my snooker repertoire. I was led out of the main bungalow to a *rondavel,* or round grass-roofed hut. It must have been just over twelve feet in diameter, because each of the four corner pockets of the snooker table touched the circular side wall.

When the time came to play, quite a crowd assembled in the hut. There was the farmer who had engaged me to play, his wife and family, a couple of dogs, and, usually under the table, a Welsh snooker professional struggling to get from one side of the hall to the other for his next shot. I certainly earned my bath that night.

IT'S A
KNOCKOUT

There is no knowing where it all began, but we can be sure that if snooker gets much more popular the Russians will claim they invented it. I should not be surprised to learn that they already have a secret Snooker Academy, probably near some deep-frozen city like Novosibirsk, where they are busy turning out dozens of 'grand masters' in preparation for a massed assault in the late 1980s on the Derby Assembly Rooms. Never mind. We shall be ready for them!

As for snooker's glorious and ancient past, there are as many theories as there are books on the subject. Billiards came first, of course, and has been traced back as far as the 6th century BC. That's too far for me. I prefer to start in more modern times, with Louis XI. He was King of France from 1461 to 1483, and he had the sense to see that all those games his people had recently taken to playing with sticks, balls and hoops, needed sorting out. There was a primitive kind of golf, and pall mall which was the forerunner of croquet, and several others. The game he liked most was billiards (or *billard*, as he called it) and the greatest achievement of his reign, no question, was to bring billiards in from the windy palace lawns and set the game up in the warm, on top of a table. There's civilization for you.

In early billiards the table contained hoops and obstacles. The balls had to pass through the hoops and avoid knocking down the obstacles, which came in various shapes such as ivory pegs, forts and castles. Some tables had pockets, others did not. Instead of the modern cue, players had upward-curving sticks with flat-ended heads which they slid across the playing surface to strike the ball.

SKITTLES POOL

The obstacles on the early billiard tables call to mind a whole family of other games. Perhaps the best-known of these is the pub game of bar billiards, where you aim to knock the balls into scoring holes; in addition, you have to avoid knocking over the skittles placed in front of the highest-scoring holes.

In my younger days in Tredegar we had a gambling game called skittles pool. Fourteen or fifteen players could join in at any one time, and (first things first) the stake was sixpence each. The money from these starting stakes, plus any further cash laid out to buy new 'lives' during a game, was put into one of the pockets, suitably lined, and the winner took all. The order of play was determined by drawing numbers from a bag.

On the table were twelve skittles, ten white and two black, and three billiard balls – white, spot-white and red. From baulk, the first player had to hit the red with his white ball and then knock down one or more white skittles. If he was successful, he scored the value of the skittle or skittles, plus the value of a numbered marble which he drew from a special container. The second player then aimed the other white ball out of baulk at either of the other two – and on to a skittle. From there, play went round the table, with white and spot-white alternating as the cue ball. Each player had one turn at a time, and the winner was the first to reach 31 exactly.

If a player went over 31, or potted a ball, or knocked down a black skittle, he lost a life. To stay in the game, he could buy a new life – provided he announced his intention before the next player took his turn; he then restarted with no points. The main art of this devious game, apart from hitting the object ball and the skittle you wanted, was to keep the players in front of you guessing about the next skittle you were aiming for, otherwise they could leave you in a hopeless position.

It was possible to break and get out with no other player hitting a ball. If, for example, you knocked down the 5 and 10 skittles, then drew the 16 marble from the bag, you were home. Thank you very much. Seven and sixpence in the pocket. On the other hand, if you were on five bob a week pocket money – as I was – and played ten games without winning, you were skint for the rest of the week.

ME AND MY CUE

Ihave recently spent eighteen months in the
doldrums, all because of a cue. One day, nearly
two years ago, my old cue broke. It was a simple
case of wear and tear; about four inches at the
top end snapped off. There was no repairing it, so
I started to look for a new one.

The old cue and I had been together for thirty years.
When I played, I didn't need to think about the cue, it worked as a
natural extension of my arm. I knew, automatically, how hard to hit the
ball; what side to put on, and how much; how much backspin; topspin;
reverse side. Everything flowed. With the new cue, I had to go back to
the beginning.

I tried several cues at first, and each one had its good
days. But none was particularly consistent. I thought it was me that
was at fault, then I found my present cue which gave me a better run of
results. I decided I would concentrate on it. A year and a half later, I
knew I had got the feel of it, and my game has been returning to what it
was.

How can a piece of wood make that much difference?
Precisely because everything about it is different from the last piece of
wood I was using. The weight distribution, for a start. That was
different. So was the way it played. I had to work out, for every shot,
how hard to hit the ball and how much swing to allow for when playing
stun shots and hitting it with side. (Contrary to what many people
think, the ball does not then travel straight, it goes in an arc.) Another
point: the new cue is an inch longer than the old one, but I decided that,
since it was a stranger to me in so many other ways, I would leave it as
it was and adapt to it. Also, it is bent.

There is a popular belief that cues must be straight.
That is why, when a player does not have his own cue with him, say at an
exhibition match, and has to select one out of the rack, the next thing he
does is roll it on the table to see if it is straight. Quite often the cue is not
straight – particularly if it is one of those Taiwanese jobs that won't
burn either – and the player says:

'Can't play with that. It's not straight.'

Then I roll my warped cue along the table. It goes
bomp–bomp–bomp. I say, accusingly:

'This table's not straight.'

The club officials love this, of course. But my reason
for doing it is not to make their life a misery, it's to quash the idea that
all cues must be straight. The truth, you might say, is not in the trueness
of the cue, it's in the way you and the cue get on together.

Thankfully, the new cue and I now get on very well.
In fact I get quite cross with anyone who wants to handle it. A lot of
people come up after a tournament and, if they
can get near it, start stroking the cue and digging
their fingernails into the tip, presumably to see if
it's real. To them I say: 'Look, you can take my wife
out, but you can't take my cue!' You think I
don't mean it?

**I remember when you
used to look at me
like that!**

TWO WEEKS IN THE LIFE

Now that we have breakfast television, I only hope we don't have to take up breakfast snooker. In an earlier chapter, on Body Maintenance, I described some of the hectic dashes that a typical pro has to make from one venue to the next. Since writing that chapter, I have fresh news to report: it's getting worse!

Now I need a driver to help me cover the ground. Without him I would be waking up in Cornwall when I should be in Glasgow. To give you an idea of how crazy our schedules can get, this is what happened to me in the two weeks after the last Benson & Hedges tournament.

SUNDAY

Play in the final, at the Conference Centre, Wembley. After the match, it's time for the television and radio interviews, the press conference, the autograph signing (a heavy session, forty-five minutes), by which time it's....

MONDAY

Get into the reception at last, celebrate with the sponsors and their guests, other players and friends. Fortunately the hotel is just across the road, so no driving. Bed at 2.30 am. Sleep. Wake to the sound of pouring rain. I am due to open a snooker centre in Holborn at midday, so pull on clothes and prepare to leave. There has been an accident on the A40, and we end up reaching the City via Neasden. Arrive at 12.30 after two hours on the road, talk to press, give instant impressions of new centre ('Very nice'), knock the inaugural ball, light lunch (no alcohol), leave at 3.30.

Head north, for Nottingham, to play Alex Higgins in an exhibition match at Bingham, which I eventually find is eight or ten miles to the east of Nottingham. Play from 7.30 until midnight. Socialize.

TUESDAY

Bingham is a two o'clock job. Back to the Post House at Sandiacre, on the M1. Very handy for the day's journey, a mere sprint down to St Albans, in Hertfordshire, which I had gone whizzing past the day before. Meet publisher (of this book) at four o'clock, have talk, go with publisher to club in St Albans where I am due to play. Club is strictly all-male, so publisher goes and brings a female with him; female accepted, I am glad to say.

WEDNESDAY

St Albans is a three o'clock job. Short sleep, then north again, to be in Carlisle at 1pm for a half-hour whistle-stop at a farmer's lunch. Imagine being in your right mind and agreeing to travel three hundred miles to chat to a bunch of blokes for thirty minutes. Justify it on the grounds that I am due next in Liverpool, where I am engaged to play that evening in a private house. Do so, then drive back to Carlisle.

THURSDAY

Wake up at noon in Carlisle hotel. Yesterday I was on the road for 9½ hours, but today I am neatly placed for the next leg to Glasgow, where I am booked to open two snooker clubs over two days. Scottish hospitality proves well up to the mark. Mind you, I like whisky. I like the water as well. In fact, I think I like the water even more, and just take a little whisky to colour it.

SATURDAY

To Yarborough Leisure Centre, Lincoln, for an exhibition match.

SUNDAY

Thinks: I'll go home today. See if the family is still there. Do so. They are. So is the dog, who bites me; he can never quite remember who I am.

MONDAY

Home is near Stoke. Get up from *own bed*, drive to Ollerton, on the other side of Mansfield – not so very far from Lincoln where I've just been. Play an exhibition. But now . . . good times are coming.

TUESDAY

Arrive in Cornwall for three days at the St Mellion Golf and Country Club. Weather sunny but cold. I cannot play golf in the cold, my fingers go numb. From bedroom window, I watch others play golf; have good laugh.

FRIDAY

Back on the road, four and a half hours up through England and over to West Wales. Route much easier for crows. Play the match. Socialize. Drive three and a half hours through the night.

SATURDAY

Arrive home at 4am. Sleep. Set off for Mansfield, to begin play at 2pm, then restart at 7.30, playing Alex Higgins in the final of a four-man tournament. Win tournament. Socialize. Go home.

So, that was a fortnight to remember. Or, you might say, one that is best forgotten. If I didn't keep a diary, I expect I would have forgotten much of it. Certainly, it would have been impossible to attempt it without a driver. Good old Derek. It's lucky he lives in Stoke too – otherwise he might never get home at all!